Nora The Piano Cat's Guide To Becoming A Good Musician

OR HOW TO GET GOOD AT ANYTHING HARD

Copyright © 2008
by Betsy Alexander and Burnell Yow!
NORA THE PIANO CAT, LLC
2301 Naudain Street
Philadelphia, PA 19146
www.ravenswingstudio.com

All photographs Copyright © 2008 by Burnell Yow!.
Cover design and layout by Burnell Yow!.

The painting *The Pride of Burnell and Betsy* by Eleanor Day
is reproduced with the kind permission of the artist.

All rights reserved, including the right to reproduce this book
or portions thereof in any form whatsoever.

For more information contact Betsy or Burnell at
info@ravenswingstudio.com

Printed and bound in the United States of America.

– Dedication –

This book is dedicated to my humans Betsy and Burnell, without whose love, care and devotion (and the occasional visit to the vet), I could never have become the good musician I am today.

Nora The Piano Cat's Guide To Becoming A Good Musician

– *Contents* –

Acknowledgments	9
About the Author	11
Introduction	13
1 - Picking an Instrument	15
2 - The Importance of Developing Your Ear	17
3 - Music is a Sport	19
4 - How Much You Need to Practice	23
5 - The Importance of Patience	25
6 - How Playing a Musical Instrument Makes You Super Smart	27

7 - The Importance of Being Kind to Yourself   29

8 - Rewarding Yourself for Your Hard Work   31

9 - How to Be Your Own Personal Best Musician   33

10 - Nora's Best-Kept Secret   35

11 - Nora's Philosophy   37

Portrait of Burnell, Betsy, and the cats by artist Eleanor Day. That's me lying on my side on the left of the image.

– *Acknowledgments* –

I'd like to thank the individuals who, directly or indirectly, made this book possible. To Burnell, for his wonderful design and layout, including the marvelous cover and the photographs. To Sarra and Jan, for their thoughtful edits and feedback. To my siblings, Clara, Miro, Gabby (who watches me like a hawk, or is always on hand to finagle a treat whenever I get one), Rennie, my one true feline friend, for providing me with playful distractions between my intense practice sessions, and to my nemesis, Max, who keeps me on my toes by providing me with plenty of opportunity to hone my Diva-ness, as well as keeping my voice in top form. To my grammy Harriet, whom I know respects me as an artist even though she is frightened of cats. And to Betsy's students for not only allowing me to learn by observing their lessons, but also for their patience, understanding, and encouragement when I "sat in" on many of their lessons.

And, of course, my sincere thanks to my mentor Betsy, whose love of music and philosophy of teaching has inspired both my playing and the very creation of this book. It didn't hurt, certainly, that she has two grand pianos and a piano bench just my size.

Last but not least, I'd like to express my sincere and deepest appreciation for all humans who, like Burnell and Betsy, have adopted or will adopt a cat from a shelter. As a cat adopted from an animal shelter whose mother was a stray, I know that although not all cats can play the piano, we *all* need a loving home.

Note: Betsy asked me to also extend her personal thanks to her teacher Barbara for inspiring her to become a better pianist and teacher. And to her teacher Helena, who taught her that by teaching, creating, and healing, we can help ourselves and others achieve our remarkable human potential.

– About the Author –

Nora The Piano Cat is a grey bull's-eye tabby and an internationally known pianist. Videos of her playing the piano have been viewed by millions of people all over the world.

She has been featured on *The Today Show, Martha Stewart, Oprah, CNN, Animal Planet* and on many other television programs in many countries. She has also been the subject of a 30 minute episode of BBC's *Extraordinary Animals*, which included an interview with cat behaviorist Beth Adelman. Ms. Adelman spent the day with Nora during the filming of the episode in Nora's home in Philadelphia, PA, during which she referred to Nora as the "P.T. Barnum of cats."

Nora's popularity extends beyond her home shores to include countries like Japan, the UK, Australia, Canada, Romania, the United Arab Emirates and many others.

Nora is the proud recipient of a DogCatemy Award from the North Shore Animal League, as well as a signed photo from Billy Joel with the inscription "To the piano cat from the piano man" and a bust of Bach presented to her by Martha Stewart. She is a self-taught musician, and her instrument of choice is a Yamaha Grand Piano.

Though she originally lived at an animal shelter in Cherry Hill, New Jersey, she now resides in Philadelphia, PA, with five cat siblings and her two personal assistants, Burnell Yow! and Betsy Alexander.

– *Introduction* –

Hello to all my human fans and a warm meow to my fellow furry felines. I want to thank each and every one of you for your interest in my piano playing. I am frequently asked how a simple cat like me became such an accomplished musician. I have given this a lot of thought and I have decided to share my wisdom with you through this little book – *Nora The Piano Cat's Guide To Becoming A Good Musician*. I hope you enjoy reading it as much as I enjoyed writing it.

Nora
2008

Nora The Piano Cat's Guide To Becoming A Good Musician

1
Picking an Instrument

I believe playing an instrument should be a part of everyone's life. It makes you smarter. It helps you develop patience, concentration and perseverance. And, of course, there is the sheer joy of expressing your inner creative spirit! That is why I can't help but purr when I play.

Unfortunately, even for a talented cat like me, there is no easy way to become a good musician – or dancer, or artist, or athlete, for that matter. To master something, anything actually, requires practice and time. You might ask, "Why spend all of that time learning an instrument when I can just listen to music on my iPod?" Well, all I can tell you is that playing is very different from listening. When I play Bach on the piano I feel like I am Bach. Like he is right there inside of me. And it is an amazing feeling, indeed – quite unlike what I feel when just listening to his music on my iPod. I feel very smart and happy when I do this. So, I am also going to share with you some of the secrets of my success as a musician in the hopes that these ideas will help you to become a good musician.

First of all, you need to pick your instrument. It was easy for me to choose the piano. That's because there were already two pianos in my house. And I especially like the way you can play more than one note at a time using both paws. I also realized, for example, that the flute would be very difficult for me. How would I hold it? And I didn't think I could develop the proper lip position to play a brass instrument.

I did, however, seriously contemplate plucking the guitar with my teeth or playing the drum with my tail. But early on I realized that playing in a band or orchestra was not for me. While you can make friends playing music with other people, for me it was out of the question. Why? Because I don't like crowds, nor do I enjoy going out. I prefer to be in the spotlight as a soloist.

2
The Importance of Developing Your Ear

I was very lucky. I got to hear Bach and Beethoven every day from when I was a tiny kitten. That's because I live with Betsy, who is a piano teacher, her husband and five annoying cat siblings. So I had the best ear training possible. I heard my favorite pieces over and over again from the moment I came home from the shelter.

Once you decide to learn an instrument, it is very important to listen to lots of music. You can go to concerts and you can listen on your iPod to pieces you want to learn. For example, if you want to play a piece by Bach (one of my favorite composers) you can download different performers playing the same piece from iTunes. That way you will know what the music should sound like and you'll become aware of the different ways the performers play the piece. You could even go to YouTube.com and watch me in action for inspiration. Or you could watch people playing the same piece you want to learn. And, of course, your teacher can play the piece for you, too.

3
Music is a Sport

When I was just a tiny kitten, I noticed the way Betsy's students sat at the piano. She spends quite a bit of time in the beginning showing her students how to sit correctly. They sit up tall and far enough away so their arms can move easily up and down the keyboard. Why is this so important, you might ask.

Well, you may not know this, but learning to play an instrument is very much like learning to play a sport. You probably already know it is important to hold a bat the right way in baseball and swing a club the right way in golf. Ice skaters must learn how to jump correctly. Basketball players must learn to bounce the ball and move at the same time.

When you go to a sports event or watch the Olympics on television, you see people who have worked very hard for a very long time to make their bodies do something difficult. You also have to train your body when you learn to play a musical instrument.

When playing the piano, just like Betsy's students, I must sit tall and use my paws correctly. I concentrate on remaining relaxed, yet strong, and using my body weight to play the notes. Millions of people have watched me on YouTube, and all of the professionals compliment me on my gentle tone. This is because I release the key instead of pounding on it, thanks to my super sensitive cat hearing.

You see, the piano is really in the drum family, and the way I press the key will determine how the note sounds. And just like a professional athlete, I must practice as often as I can or I will not be able to play my best. To control my paws, or in your case, ten different fingers, requires playing the same thing over and over until it gets easy. Those of you who ride skateboards, horses, or bicycles know exactly what I am talking about.

Nobody rides a two-wheel bicycle without first trying training wheels and then practicing. No one does fancy jumps with their skateboard the first time they try it. And no one plays fancy music the first time they try.

I know I may make it look easy, but as Nora The Piano Cat, that's what I'm supposed to do. Great performers like me want to share their art with their audience. We do not want you to think about how hard it is for us. We just want you to concentrate on the beauty of the music and have a good time. But ask any good pianist or athlete you know how much they practice and I guarantee you their response will be that they practice quite a bit. Did you know that some concert pianists practice 6 hours a day? They do this because they need to be very strong if they want to play the most difficult music.

They are just like baseball players who must go to spring training before baseball season. Think about it. A ballet dancer or an Olympic ice skater may make it look easy, but we all know they have worked very hard to get good and stay good at what they do. Now I'm not saying you have to be a famous musician like me. Lots of people play instruments for their own enjoyment. Some people have more time to practice than others. All I'm saying is, the more time you put into it and the more you practice, the faster you will progress.

Nora The Piano Cat's Guide To Becoming A Good Musician

4
How Much You Need to Practice

Some of you may be lucky to find 10 or 20 minutes to practice playing your instrument several times a week. Others may lump it all together the night before their lesson (not ideal – but it's better than not learning at all!). Ultimately, the important thing is to just stick with it. If you keep playing, you will eventually get better and better.

I have been practicing every day since I was one year old. Many people have asked me how, as a cat with so many different interests and fans to keep in touch with, I manage to practice everyday, especially on days when I am not in the mood. I use several different techniques.

On days when I am more interested in catnaps or playing with my yellow feather, I tell myself: "Just sit down and play one piece" or, "Just play for 5 minutes." Usually, I play way longer than I thought I would. Sometimes, though, I just play my one piece, or just play for 5 minutes. And that is OK with me. If I'm having a bad day, I still feel proud that I sat down and played a bit.

5
The Importance of Patience

I know it's hard to believe but sometimes when I am trying to learn a hard part of the music, I get very frustrated. We all do – beginners and concert pianist cats alike. It doesn't matter. We are all trying to do something that is difficult for us.

Learning to play an instrument is a good way to learn to do difficult things. And this is a very good lesson because life is full of challenges. Take catching a bug or a mouse, for instance. It is not easy for cats to hunt but we never give up. And when we finally catch something, boy do we feel great! I have the same terrific feeling when I get good at a hard part of a piece of music.

There is no need to waste your valuable time playing the easy parts over and over. Go straight to the hardest parts. The harder they are, the smaller and simpler you need to make them. I always play the hard parts one paw at a time, and I try to play them very slowly so my cat brain and paws will learn them as quickly as possible. Although I sometimes find slow, careful playing a little boring, it really does work.

If I play something fast and wrong over and over, it never seems to get better. And that's the whole point isn't it – to get better?

6
How Playing a Musical Instrument Makes You Super Smart

My cat brain, and your human brain, is like an amazing computer. When I want a better computer, however, I can go out and buy one. But if I want a bigger or faster brain, the only way I can get it is by doing things that are hard for me, and by doing them over and over until they feel easy. This is how I grow my brain, and this is why playing the piano has helped me become a smarter cat.

You see, when you try to play something difficult, your brain needs to grow a new brain connection. When the hard part finally feels easier, it is because you grew a new brain connection by playing it again and again. You can almost feel it happening. One minute it feels like your brain is going to explode, the next minute you suddenly understand the thing that seemed so hard. And that means not only are you better at the piano, but you are smarter than you were before you started.

And guess what? It is never too early or too late to learn an instrument or a new piece of music. Betsy has students as young as 2 and as old as 72. Learning something new is good for you no matter what age you are.

How cool is that?

7
The Importance of Being Kind to Yourself

Sometimes I have to remind myself to be patient and kind to my paws, because my smart cat brain often understands the music before my paws do. It can feel frustrating when my paws won't do what my brain knows. but I also know it is unlikely that you'll learn something new without making mistakes at first. In fact, if you are not making mistakes, you are probably *not* trying to do something new.

You also need to have a sense of humor and adventure. Betsy even made up a word for those times when one feels confused and overwhelmed. I can't tell you how many times I have heard her say to her students "I think you are a bit 'mishkabibbled'. Just try it again." This makes them laugh. They seem to know exactly what she means, and they don't feel mad about making a mistake. They just take it in stride. Making mistakes is just part of the learning process. So, when you get *mishkabibbled*, just laugh and try it again!

8
Rewarding Yourself for Your Hard Work

I think it is a good idea to reward yourself for your efforts. I especially like cat treats and I love stickers – fuzzy stickers, glittery stickers, you name it.

If you want, you can make a chart with a picture of me on it to inspire you, then put a check mark or sticker on it each time you practice or when you get good at something. You can even make up little contests, like how many days can you practice in a row or how many minutes can you practice in a month.

When you achieve your goal, you can celebrate. I like to have some catnip or a play session with my brother, Rennie, but you could order a pizza or go out to a favorite place. You decide. Give yourself something to look forward to, and working hard to reach your goals will be more fun.

9

How to Be Your Own Personal Best Musician

When learning to play an instrument, it is so important to focus on yourself and your own progress. Learning to play the piano is easier for some people than it is for others. In my case, I certainly wouldn't compare my playing to Betsy's. She is a human. I am a cat. She has 10 fingers. I only have two paws (and my head) to use to play the notes. So, our progress is very different. And our music is very different. Betsy has a human attention span and, of course, I have a cat's. The slightest noise or movement distracts me, and I have to stop what I'm doing and check it out. I just can't help it. Obviously, this affects the quality of my practice time.

But I never compare myself to Betsy and her human students. I am proud to be a cat pianist, and very pleased with what I have achieved. I compete only with myself and I don't worry about what other people or cats are doing. After all, I play the piano for my own reasons and for personal enjoyment. I like who I am, because I am the best cat I can be.

Now that doesn't mean I don't enjoy hearing another talented human or cat pianist. In fact, I am inspired by other good musicians. But that is certainly different than comparing myself to them. For example, Betsy can never hope to achieve my level of international fame, but she is not the least bit bothered by this. She knows there is room for all kinds of music and musicians in this world, amateur and professional alike.

10
Nora's Best-Kept Secret

It really doesn't matter if it takes you six weeks or six months or six years to learn your Bach piece. All that matters is that you get better at it and enjoy playing the piece once you are good at it. No one cares or knows how long it took you to learn your piece. They just enjoy listening to you play it. In fact, they might think it took you only six minutes to learn your piece because you play it so beautifully.

How long it really took and just how hard it was can be our little secret!

Nora The Piano Cat's Guide To Becoming A Good Musician

Asa with Nora - Photo by Betsy

11
Nora's Philosophy

One of the most wonderful things you learn from studying a musical instrument is that through our hardest challenges we grow the most. And once you understand this, life becomes much more fun and exciting.

I also believe we were put on this planet to create things. It is our natural ability. We are all musicians, artists, and gardeners at heart. That is what it means to be alive.

Betsy even thinks everyone can write music, and I'm inclined to agree. After all, I like to meow, and all children like to hum little tunes – isn't that composing? We all have many abilities and talents hidden within us. Who would have thought it was possible, for instance, for a cat to play the piano. And look at me now! I am world-famous!

Take it from me, Nora The Piano Cat, you just have to be willing to try.

Visit Nora's website and blog at:
www.ravenswingstudio.com/NoraWeb/nora_news

Or email her at:
norapianocat@ravenswingstudio.com

Made in the USA